MAMA CAN YOU TEACH ME?

Michele Gmitrowski

Copyright © 2020 Michele Gmitrowski.

Cover and Interior design by Michele Gmitrowski

This is a short story children's book

All rights reserved. No part of this book may be reproduced or used in any manner without written permission of the copyright owner except for the use of quotations in a book review.

This Book is Dedicated

To All My Grandchildren

You all gave me the inspiration to

Write my very first children's book

Thank you,

Love, Nana

Mama, can you teach me?

I want to dance like you

Show me how to put my feet

And dress me just like you.

Do my hands go up like this?

Do I bend my knees too?

Mama what is that you're wearing?

"It's called a Tutu"...

TUTU

Mama can I wear one so

I can look like you?

Oh this is so pretty it

is the same as yours

Mama, oh you did my hair

I want to shout "Yahoo"

When I am playing by myself

I twirl and jump with joy

I pretend that I am you, Mama,

When you jump it is so high

Sometimes when I watch you...

it's like your going to touch the sky

Mama, do I look pretty?

I want to look like you

Oh Mama!, when I look in the mirror I think I am seeing you...

www.ingramcontent.com/pod-product-compliance
Lightning Source LLC
Chambersburg PA
CBHW051307110526
44589CB00025B/2961